Contents

Use your hands!..............4

Rough and smooth..........6

Super skin!....................8

Hot and cold................10

Wet and dry.................12

Hard and soft...............14

Slimy and prickly...........16

Arts and crafts..............18

Friends together...........20

Notes for adults...........22

Index...........................24

Touching and Feeling

CENT

J

Katie Dicker

First published in paperback 2011,
by Evans Brothers Limited
2A Portman Mansions
Chiltern Street
London W1U 6NR

Produced for Evans Brothers Limited by
White-Thomson Publishing Ltd

Printed by Everbest in China
July 2011, job number (CAG1678)
Printed on chlorine-free paper from sustainably managed sources.

Educational consultant: Sue Palmer MEd FRSA FEA
Project manager: Katie Dicker
Picture research: Amy Sparks
Design: Balley Design Limited
Creative director: Simon Balley
Designer/Illustrator: Michelle Tilly/Andrew Li

The activities in this book are designed to be used at the discretion of the pre-school
practitioner, teacher or parent/guardian. The publisher shall not be liable for any
accidents, losses or malpractices arising from or relating to these activities.

British Library Cataloguing in Publication Data

Dicker, Katie
  Touching and feeling. - (My senses) (Sparklers)
  1. Touch - Pictorial works - Juvenile literature
  I. Title
  612.8'8

ISBN: 978 0 2375 4450 8

What do you like to touch with your hands?

tickles!

5

Rough and smooth

rough ridges

Shells can feel rough and bumpy.

This **sand** is **gritty** but **smooth** to **touch**.

Super Skin!

You can *feel* things all over your body.

8

What does water feel like on your skin?

Hot and cold

ouch!

The sun has warmed this sand.

It feels very hot!

kapow!

In winter, the snow feels cold and powdery.

Wet and dry

splash!

Max is clean but soaking wet.

12

Hard and soft

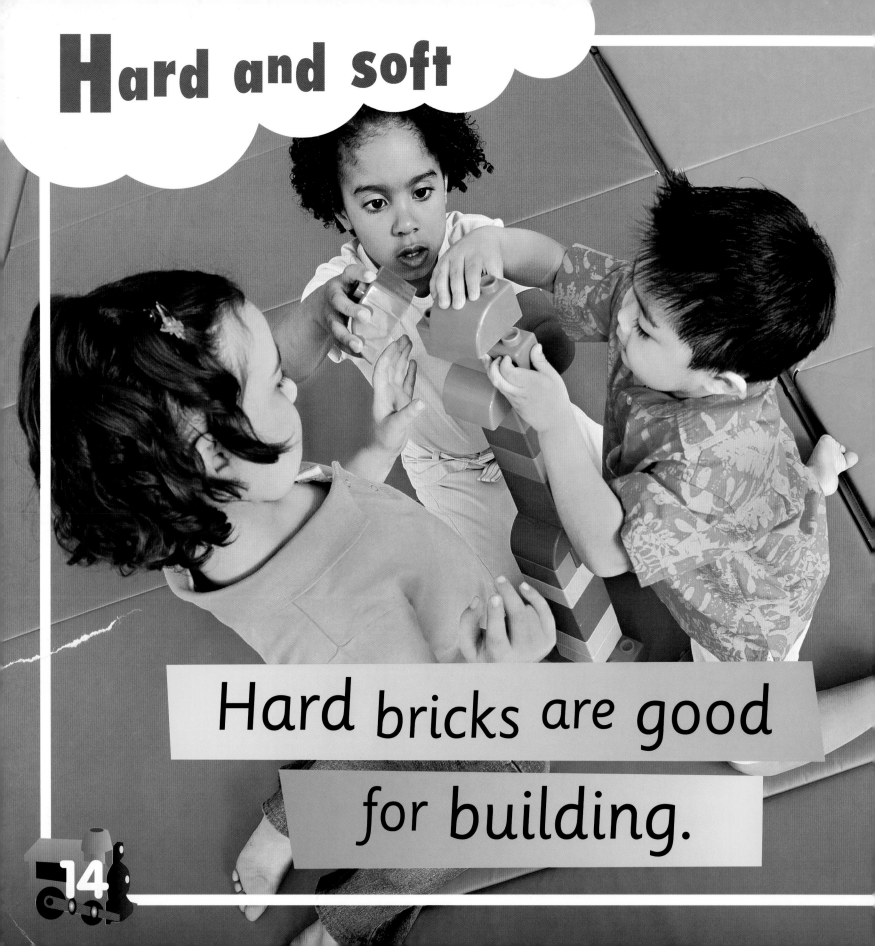

Hard bricks are good for building.

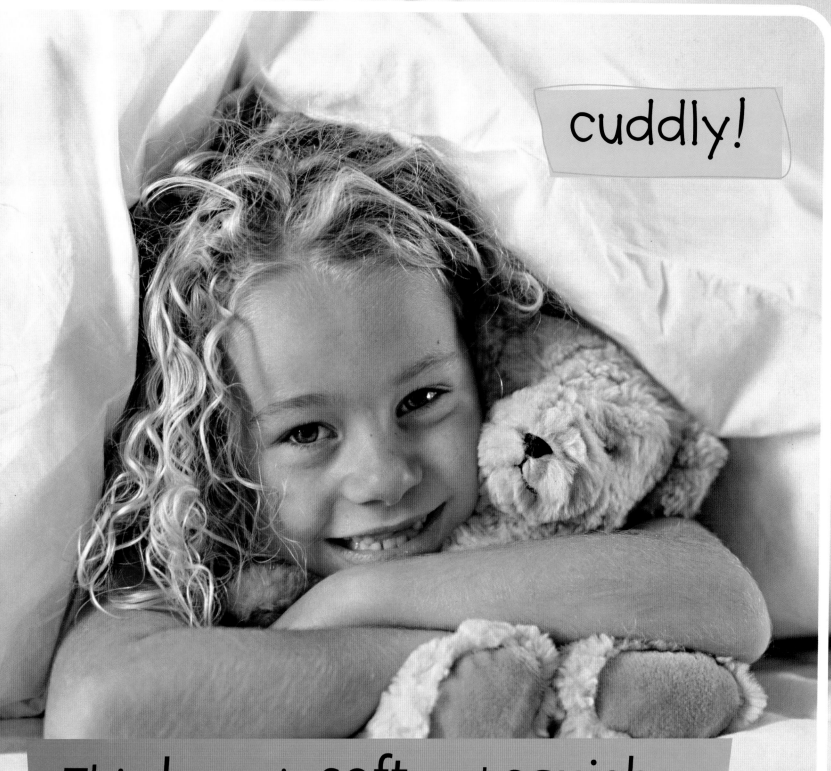

cuddly!

This bear is soft and squishy.

Slimy and prickly

slippery!

A snail feels really slimy.

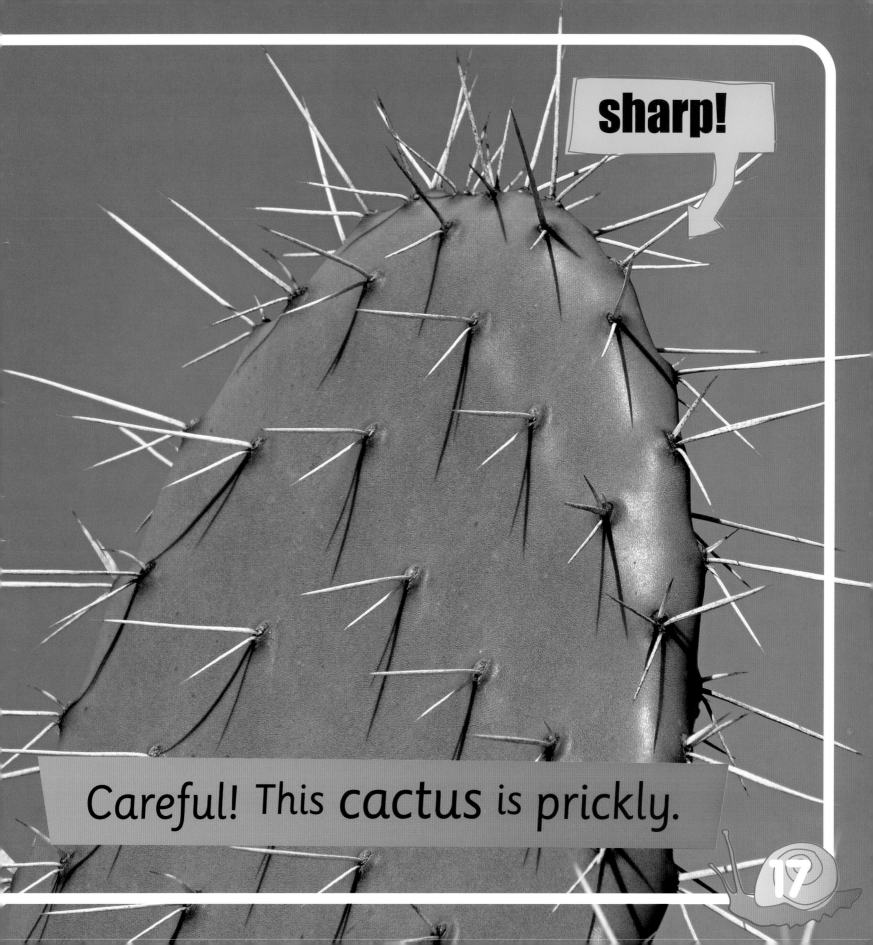

sharp!

Careful! This **cactus** is prickly.

17

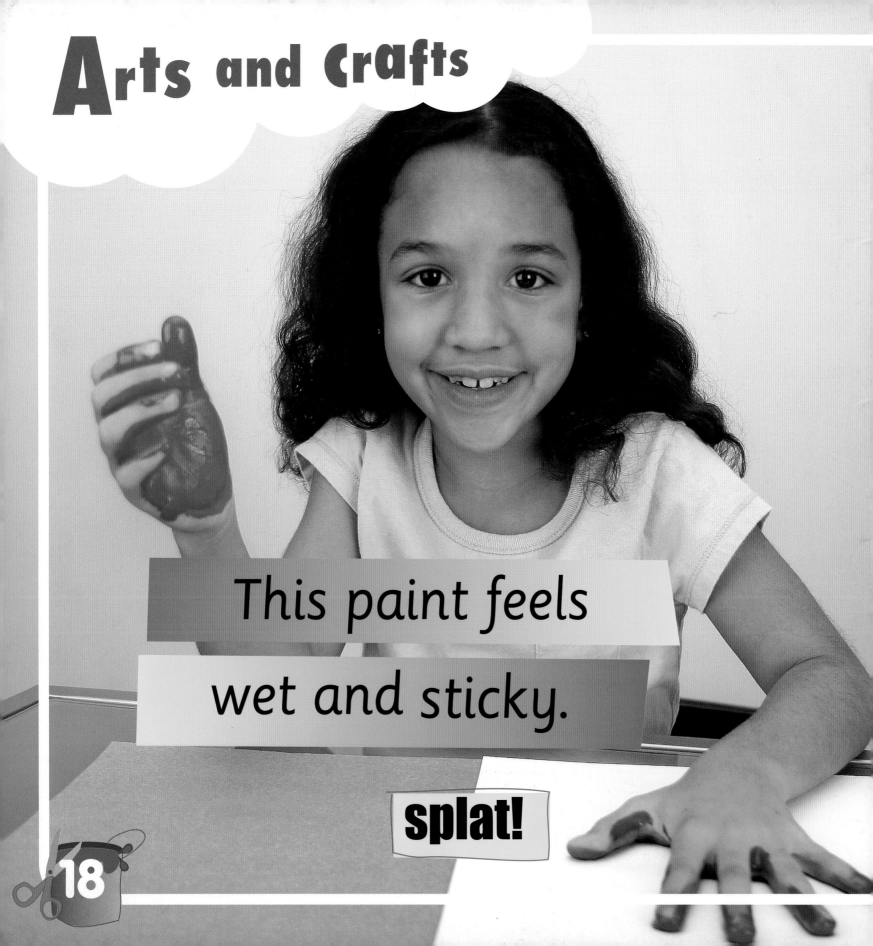

This paint feels

wet and sticky.

splat!

steady!

Amit makes his robot tall and strong.

Friends together

We hold hands to show we are friends.

A hug can *feel* even **better!**

21

Notes for adults

Sparklers books are designed to support and extend the learning of young children. The **Food We Eat** titles won a Practical Pre-School Silver Award, the **Body Moves** titles won a Practical Pre-School Gold Award and the **Out and About** titles won the 2009 Practical Pre-School Gold Overall Winner Award. The books' high-interest subjects link in to the Early Years Foundation Stage curriculum and beyond. Find out more about Early Years and reading with children from the National Literacy Trust (www.literacytrust.org.uk).

Themed titles
Touching and Feeling is one of four **Senses** titles that explore the five senses of sight, touch, smell, taste and sound. The other titles are:

Seeing   **Hearing**   **Tasting and Smelling**

Areas of learning
Each **Senses** title helps to support the following Foundation Stage areas of learning:
Personal, Social and Emotional Development
Communication, Language and Literacy
Mathematical Development
Knowledge and Understanding of the World
Physical Development
Creative Development

Making the most of reading time
When reading with younger children, take time to explore the pictures together. Ask children to find, identify, count or describe different objects. Point out colours and textures. Allow quiet spaces in your reading so that children can ask questions or repeat your words. Try pausing mid-sentence so that children can predict the next word. This sort of participation develops early reading skills.

Follow the words with your finger as you read. The main text is in Infant Sassoon, a clear, friendly font designed for children learning to read and write. The labels and sound effects add fun and give the opportunity to distinguish between levels of communication. Where appropriate, labels, sound effects or main text may be presented phonically. Encourage children to imitate the sounds.

As you read the book, you can also take the opportunity to talk about the book itself with appropriate vocabulary such as "page", "cover", "back", "front", "photograph", "label" and "page number".

You can also extend children's learning by using the books as a springboard for discussion and further activities. There are a few suggestions on the facing page.

Pages 4–5: Use your hands!

Fill a dark bag with different items of food, such as fruit, wrapped sweets or nuts and pass the bag around a group of children. Ask each child to touch an item without looking at it, and to describe it to the group. Children could try identifying the feel of objects using different parts of their body, too. Discuss why the hands are so sensitive and which parts of the body do not sense feeling (such as cutting your hair or your nails).

Pages 6–7: Rough and smooth

Children may enjoy doing 'texture rubbings'. Collect a variety of shells or leaves for the children to work with. Place each shell or leaf under a sheet of thin paper and gently rub the paper with a dark-coloured crayon. An image of the shell/leaf will begin to appear. Ask the children to identify which parts of the shell/leaf are rough and which are smooth.

Pages 8–9: Super skin!

Children may enjoy collecting different materials – such as feathers, pipe cleaners and wool – and to test what they feel like on their skin. The children could take part in a competition to see who is the least ticklish. Which parts of the body are the most ticklish? Are the children able to tickle themselves?

Pages 10–11: Hot and cold

Encourage children to explore the feeling of different temperatures. Fill a bowl with iced water, a bowl of tepid water and a bowl of hand-hot water. Ask the children to put their left hand in the iced water and their right hand in the hand-hot water. Then ask them to put their left hand in the tepid water. What does it feel like? Now add their right hand to the tepid water. What does it feel like this time?

Pages 12–13: Wet and dry

Collect a sample of different materials or clothes (such as cotton, wool, velvet, denim and plastic). Encourage children to describe what the materials feel like. Then ask the children to soak the materials in water and hang them up to dry. Check the materials after 2 hours and then again the following day. Which materials take longest to dry? Which materials are waterproof?

Pages 14–15: Hard and soft

Collect a series of hard or soft blocks of different sizes. Ask the children to arrange the blocks in their order of size, while blindfolded. How many do they get right? Children may also enjoy playing games while blindfolded, such as 'braille dominoes', a texture maze or a simple jigsaw puzzle.

Pages 16–17: Slimy and prickly

Make a series of texture cards by gluing substances (such as sand, flour, seeds, rice and glitter) to different cards. You could use materials such as corrugated card and bubble wrap, too. Encourage children to feel the cards while blindfolded and to describe and identify what they are touching.

Pages 18–19: Arts and crafts

Children may enjoy painting with different tools, to get a sense of different types of textures. Tools could include their finger, a sponge, a toothbrush, a potato, a cork or a pipe cleaner.

Pages 20–21: Friends together

Ask children to think about all the ways they have used their sense of touch today. What activities would they have found difficult if they could not feel? Which types of touch helped them to communicate their feelings and emotions?

Index

c
cold **11**

d
dry **13**

f
feel **4, 6, 8, 9, 10, 11,
13, 16, 18, 21**

g
gritty **7**

h
hands **4, 5, 20**
hard **14**
hot **10**

p
powdery **11**
prickly **17**

r
rough **6**

s
sharp **17**
skin **8, 9**
slimy **16**
slippery **16**
smooth **7**
soft **15**
squishy **15**
sticky **18**
strong **19**

t
touch **5, 7**

w
warm **10**
water **9**
wet **12, 18**

Picture acknowledgements:
Corbis: 10 (Joson/zefa), 11 (Don Mason), 12 (Tom Stewart), 13 (Roger Ressmeye), 15 (Gulliver/zefa); **Getty Images:** cover (Jose Luis Pelaez), 4 (Anthony Harvie), 6 (Patrick Molnar), 7 (Sakis Papadopoulos), 8-9 (Ariel Skelley), 14 (Andersen Ross), 17 (Martin Ruegner), 19 (Ariel Skelley); **IStockphoto:** cover tablecloth (Gaffera), cover sky (Judy Foldetta), 5 (Viorika Prikhodko); **Photolibrary:** 21 (Roy Morsch); **Shutterstock:** 2-3 balls of wool (Angelo Gilardelli), 16 (Marilyn Barbone), 18 (Rob Marmion), 20 (David H. Seymour), 22-23 feathers, 24 feathers (Victoria Alexandrova).